MW01106707

This

World

We

Invented

# This World We Invented

## Carolyn Marie Souaid

*To Maurice!*
*Looking forward*
*to reading your*
*prize winning book!*
*Best,*
*Carolyn*

Brick Books

Library and Archives Canada Cataloguing in Publication

Souaid, Carolyn Marie, 1959-, author
    This world we invented / Carolyn Marie Souaid.

Poems.
Issued in print and electronic formats.
ISBN 978-1-77131-354-4 (pbk.).--ISBN 978-1-77131-356-8 (pdf).--
ISBN 978-1-77131-355-1 (epub)

    I. Title.

PS8587.O87T47 2015          C811'.54          C2014-907987-7
                                              C2014-907988-5

We acknowledge the Canada Council for the Arts, the Government of Canada through
the Canada Book Fund, and the Ontario Arts Council for their support of our publishing
program.

The author photo was taken by Endre Farkas.
The book is set in Dante.
Cover image by Gts.
Design and layout by Marijke Friesen.
Printed and bound by Sunville Printco Inc.

Brick Books
431 Boler Road, Box 20081
London, Ontario  N6K 4G6

www.brickbooks.ca

# CONTENTS

## I SKETCHBOOK

## II THIS WORLD WE INVENTED

### i

*for Endre*

# I

# SKETCHBOOK

"Concept has form."
—Kit White
(from *101 Things to Learn in Art School*)

# Scale

Africa was an inch and a half wide on my ruler.
The teacher smiled and pasted something into my book,
either a gold star or a moth with exceptional markings,
I don't recall.

She died. Lots of people died.
Push-pins came off the map, but more went in.
Overnight, the population doubled.
Where sprightly children once leapt about,
there were meaner ones
who excelled at games—

tagging a hapless ant with a magnifying glass,
harnessing the sun, funnelling it into a prick of light,
then watching the scrabbling insect shrivel
into a seed.

It was, of course, the same destiny that awaited Joshua,
whose miraculous entry into the human race began
tentatively, on a bed of straw.

It isn't any one individual per se; it's the layers
of human thought that append themselves to an idea
and set its entire life course.

Back two thousand years,
blue sky met the ochre sand
in a perfect line.
It was the wandering shepherd who triggered all the fuss—
the celebratory gesturing of his hands.

## Shape

My ex keeps asking do I want the cat back,
but my place is a wall short
and where pray tell to put the litter box?

Gets me asking other questions—
Where in the dryer does the missing sock go?
And to be dead, what's it like? Actually.

Now that I'm fifty, things don't fit so well.
My clothes, for instance.

But I'm comfortable alone
with the cold-shot chrysanthemums,
picturing myself at the bottom
of the food chain,
countless nautical miles from consciousness,

a sponge in the ancient sea
or a hairy primordial cell. Of course,
there aren't the familiar reference points.
No cities accessorized with cars.
Here, it's just me—
in a different kind of overcoat,

brainlessly adrift in the mud-filled swamp.
Algae unaware of *love* or *loss*,
words that catch in the back of the throat,

only the pulsing yes/no of being here for a time,
and then not.

# Space

Space is not neutral.
It depends on who inhabits it
and how.
Here, it's imbued with impulse.
It breathes.
It is wooded with dark creatures—
though it might just be me.
It's a dimension I'd rather not think about.
I enter anyway. Being human.
A residue of violence clings to the windowsill.
You and your wife, why did you?
And repeatedly, according to the news.
The space is not neutral.
Nor is the one embracing the crib.
The room vomited.
It bled, peed, shat.
It made gurgling baby sounds.
It screamed its lungs out.
Day and night.
The space shifted to Intensive Care.
I enter because. In a way I have to.
Now it's a tangle of circuitry.
It breathes mechanically.
In, out, in, out.
It is unresponsive to light.
Painting it would be out of the question.
Utterly.
Even thinking it.
But being human.
I'd imagine a landscape.
One long, yellowy line.
With my pencil,
        vigorously,
I'd strike it through.

## Pattern

After years of assorted forgettables,
hand-me-downs, rust buckets,
gas-guzzling, money-sucking
Skyhawks and Monzas,

when, for the first time, I see my Mazda
on the lot, brand-spanking-new,
all twenty-thousand dollars of it
without a scratch,
fenders sleek and intact,
not a spot of rust on the underbelly,
the finest feline (within my price range)
I've ever laid eyes on,
it doesn't cross my mind
I'm taking a big gamble.

I'm as cool as Catherine Deneuve
in the breaking light of dawn,
coming home from the all-night casino
in a trench coat that Bogart
or Jean-Paul Belmondo might wear,
pockets stuffed with winnings.

I don't ask.
So I don't know.

How can I possibly know
when I lay down my cash and
pull the lever,
mouth watering in anticipation,
that the spinning symbols—
three perfect lemons—
will align just like that,
propitiously?
Then, within the first month,
I'll hit the jackpot again:
rammed once,
towed twice;
and that damned skunk will leave behind
its lucky streak—
all over my faux-leather interior.

# Figure and Ground

*I go the way of all the earth.*
    —David to Solomon (1 Kings 2:2)

A guy on the outskirts of town
believes wholeheartedly in his existence.
Swears it up and down to the kid
who's tied him to the end of her string
like a balloon.
"Let me go." He's not smiling.

He should have known something was up
when the morning clock startled him awake
but left his wife intact.
He brushed his teeth and knotted a tie.
Suddenly, without warning, he was airborne,
propelled by an unidentified force
that threw him against the office door
then pinned him to the ceiling
like a common fly—

until a warm draft of industrial air sent him
through the window, and up, up
into the mothy light.

Which brings us full circle to the quarrel
with the girl in pigtails, and his pleading
to please, please release him—
(like the song).

And she agrees, cutting the string
so that across town, a graveyard registers
the quickened flutter of a heart, or hearts;
the last autumn rush of geese.

# Light

*...be happy!*
*and with your beads on, because it rains.*
  —Frank O'Hara

What good are they sleeping
in their darkish bedrooms?
I want to tell them before it's too late:

Morning, like a coral bloom,
floats on the waves.

Take out your fingerpaints,
stewards of the drifting fronds
and radiant sun along the rippled floor—

see that fishing boat at the end of the wharf?
The muck of river stones in your hand

is a good thing.

## Perspective

The birthday light across my face
is the light that flanks the pub
where my son and his pals share
a convivial pitcher of beer.
They're so young, so ultra cool.

For them, life stands impossibly still—
like a room evenly divided,
the pressure on one side of the wall
equal to the other: a zero-sum game.
They never expect the inevitable,
not at their age.

Of course, they understand it in theory.
They've memorized the beautiful/repugnant cycle
for tests: you're a cell,
you're a boy, you're a man, you're a corpse.

But what do they know?
The boundaries shift imperceptibly—

    A larval wind swoops in, and colonies
    of insects swarm the orifices
    of the dead. In the town below,
    a boisterous caravan leaves the marketplace,
    a weaving procession of camels and goats
    and turbaned men who will walk
    forty days and forty nights without sleep
    into the next century,
    where clouds liquefy into rain, as they always have,
    and seasons bleed, one into the other,
    winter to spring to summer to fall,
    massaging and hydrating the earth
    where everything breeds and multiplies.

Time intervenes.
In a busy city of black umbrellas,
Darwin reviews his notebook
of leapfrog derivations before dozing off
by candlelight, dreaming
of another millennium and a new taxonomy
of lithe cars that will please everybody
on Jupiter.

# Colour

The more we apply, the less provisional
we become. And yes, the more human.

Take the husband of the woman
with the lopped-off breasts.
Consider him the paltry spectrum
of emotional absence: iced slate, timber wolf.
Shadow.

For a decent stretch, they were in love,
the burgeoning geography of their lives
winding a sly path underfoot,
the serpentine trajectory forking ahead
as he slipped the ring, auspiciously, onto her finger.
And while the two of them stood there,
frozen in time,
everything came, everything came to them
wrapped in a brilliant department store box.
Their eyes shone,
their hearts were sprayed in ocean mist.
For years, nothing. Everything.
And then.

An unanticipated shade: plum cloud,
tropical storm, sky weighing in
as black as a pearl.
One could say with reasonable certainty
that this is where he turned.

## Chiaroscuro

For seven days and seven nights,
I waited for an air conditioner.
Ants were building a hill on my patio.
The lawn, the rooftops, cars, my pool,
everything was webbed in a powdery grit,
though I detected in the curtains
a hint of rain.

       Otherwise, my days were taken up
with a vague memory of the man
at the metro station
urging me to a Adopt-a-Kid
from some African village
like ones I've seen in glossy pictures torn
from *National Geographic*—
a sun so white it blanches the heads
of every dark child lying skeletal
in the dust, nothing on the horizon
but fire and wind,
no miracle, not a single cool drop
waiting to splash down on them.

## Symmetry

The unemployed welder
in the upstairs flat waits
each afternoon for the sluggish day
to sprout a dress and heels,
a woman lean and shapely,
nails buffed, hair a tumble of jasmine
and earth.
        The man knows.

He knows that when she glances his way,
momentarily, she'll see not the cloud
of weeds on his lawn, or
the forklike crack in his foundation.
        She will see him.

Monday through Friday, he watches
the comings and goings of the coroners
as the dying coal of his cigarette
burns down, and out.

## Context

The child, straddling her mom, bends
to the rapids,
her fingers like buds awakened
to the shaggy wind,

the metallic sprint of river water.
The ducks shoot past

and she cups her hand, wanting in.
But the mother's restraining arm
tells another story, rooted in her fears
of the disturbed ecosystem, the quagmire of
what's below or beyond

or overhead, threatening.
Even the dense clouds buttressing the sky
are unravelling, strand by strand.

## Notes on Composition

See it as a celebration of flight. Prepare to stray
outside your range of experience.

Never shoot at high noon
or during the hackneyed ends of day.

Be wary of light. Know your birds
and the peculiarities of a feeding frenzy.

Study the way the ornithologist
follows his nose, how he works

his viewfinder so the camera does the rest.
Put away the brush and wait.

You get your best material after dark.

## Collage

The first-drawn breaths,
filling the air with movement.

A green apple touches four walls
like the body at the womb
of a tree, opening itself.

Pale yarrow waves,
sprints down the street
from side to side, swaying
in the white light of eight o'clock.

I am more frightened of flowers than anything.

Every evening in the metropole
something brushes against your foot,
guides you so far.
But the heart wanders where it will.

Once, I saw you on the street and watched you
disappear,
so young, and already a genius.

The room is empty.
We are held by a moment
the colour of water.

Let me start over.

Time grew large, and then compacted.

✱

The sound of a distant siren.
Above us, night repeats itself.
Pushed by an invisible hand.
This is the entranceway.
The clock runs in either direction.

The theatre's gone, the Laundromat.
Your anger has fallen through a mirror.
I look at my palm.
It is quiet; you are warm.

✱

Maybe when I'm 90, bent beyond recognition,
eyes unable to focus, I'll tell you something.

What happened was prophesy. Repeating
a slow sad dance, up and then down.

I think of you constantly at the door, that letter
in your hand. Cold as January rain.

Such was the conceit.

The hard blue feral spark,
the sky,

a sigh erupting where stars used to be.
Stand still and you can feel time collapse.

\*

What you need to say has many rooms:

A man who smells of rotting mushrooms.
A man who may or may not own a truck.

That slide of eye, that wary glance.

August everywhere, but only
in this one meadow.

Saying *home*.
It has the weight of a stone falling.

## Shadow

You say you have faith.
But do you, after all that's happened,
still believe in a sun that taps along your spine—
just because. Do you?

Animals appeared two by two on the horizon.
A sign, you felt.
Evidence of the great
waters of the planet shifting.

Worried, you consulted the scriptures
and the ancient Babylonian horoscopes—
reminders
that after the smouldering trees,
after the last
recorded typhoons,
Earth becomes mist.

Halfway up the hill, the path runs out.

# II

# THIS WORLD WE INVENTED

"An idea is only as good as its execution."
—Kit White
(from *101 Things to Learn in Art School*)

i

## Bildungsroman

Whether you crawled out of the gel and slime of the sea
or materialized on the damp underside of a rock,
you begin the same way—
mulishly here, digging in your heels.
Trees spring up out of nowhere,
their girth widening as you take root
in the day-to-day task of making do,
wondering whether it's enough
to come and go with the seasons
or if it's true that a certain so-and-so
blinked once to put you at the confluence of rivers,
the great momentum pulling you along.

Your body loves, indiscriminately:
warm spring rain in your hair,
low-lying clouds over emerald hills.
They open your desire
for meaning, lead you through brush and fog
toward the age-old story:

out of the giant pores of Earth
comes the first iridescence. Spores and sponges,
reptiles, insects, mammals.
Eventually, their loping mutations surpass you.
Behind your back, they whisper about your rickety bones,
the dinosaur infrastructure of your brain.
But turn things around:
who these days remembers fire,
papyrus, the first Mesopotamian wheel?
Who notices the roofs all over town springing leaks,
the overflowing gutters? The planets
out of whack, out of tune, out of synch,
the cyclical sun in slow decline?

It's not theatre.
You don't cry, despite the "For Sale" sign going up
on the crumbling facade of your house
and the smug new moon moving its luggage in.
Whether you crawled out of the gel and slime of the sea
or materialized on the damp underside of a rock,
at the end of the day,
you'll be bolting out of here breathlessly.
Taking the basement steps two at a time
until the floor opens up and returns you
to the earth.

## City of Everything

City of arrivals.
City of missed connections.
City of plate glass windows shouldered in fog.
City of terminals and interminable waits.
City of Beefeater.
City of laptops and mobile devices.
City of flux.
City of escalators.
City of criss-crossed time zones.
City of no time to lose.
City of left-hand turns down a staircase of shopping bags.
City of Gucci.
City of umbrellas.
City of luggage.
City of "Excuse me, can you tell me ...?"
City of looping echo.
City of strollers.
City of wheelchairs.
City of carry on and carry off.
City of parabolic laughter, 7.5 on the Richter scale.
City of Double Wear Stay-in-Place Makeup.
City of blush.
City of Apple.
City of lithe women in arching doorways.
City of legs.
City of incubating disease.
City of extended naps and early risers.
City of day.
City of ordinary details, like the sun, repeating.
Flip-flops and hideous toes, flip-flops and hideous toes.
City of hangnails.
City of rot.
City of concrete.
City of stiff.
City of shine.

City of cufflinks.
City of shirts and business suits pressed into cardboard.
City of standby.
City of hurry up and wait.
City of beeping electric carts backing into the throng.
City of turbans and burkas and Biotherm.
City of parasites on toilet seats.
City of farts.
City of India, Poland, Spain, France, Turkey, Japan, but mainly India.
City of credit cards.
City of faulty wiring.
City of Christmas tchotchkes in October display cases.
City of grandmothers in turtlenecks.
City of convergence.
City of fragrance.
City of chocolate.
City of paper.
City of glass, chrome, lead; city of nickel.
City of neon, marble, steel.
City of hard.
City of edge.
City of nerve.
City of trench coats.
City of emergency exits.
City of maps.
City of girls going to Idaho.
City of lost in the shuffle.
City of cloying loudspeaker distortion.
City of fat.
City of broom-pushers.
City of urinals.
City of Starbucks.
City of accelerating innovation.
City of hyper.
City of connections.

City of "Stop," "Go," "Move your ass."
City of billboards.
City of blinking.
City of cancelled reservations.
City of complainers.
City of lineups.
City of corduroy, denim, suede, leather and cotton.
City of canvas.
City of vinyl.
City of rubber.
City of stretch.
City of oversized watches.
City of Made in China.
City of mustard stains.
City of buttonholes.
City of unravelling hems.
City of dharma.
City of drama.
City of who among us is dying of cancer?
City of c'mon now, which one of us?
City of weakened immunity.
City of abandon hope ye who enter here.
City of night.
City of cooled surfaces.
City of cobweb.
City of drift.
City of swirling green gas.
City of border patrols.
City of passports.
City of fog.
City of departures.

# House Front

—AFTER A PAINTING BY EMILY CARR

After the flame, what remains, scattered
among the booming trees—

a blue-black sky, tarnished with leaves,
groping shadows on an olive smudge
of trodden grass.

A tentative canoe, overturned, has no place to go.
Waits for a cue.

Like the Indian hut and its totem facade
of strangulated faces.

About the people.
They are thirsty.

A child wearing a cotton dress
leans into the mountain strength
of her father.
God has disappeared entirely.
A ghost of laundry floats in the wind.

## Seagulls

Outside my window,
in the parking lot of the Arabic grocery store,
a hundred seagulls assemble
to avoid the sharpshooting wind off the highway.
The clouds are low down and on the offensive.

*Hup two, three, four. Hup two, three, four.*
The cockiest male struts
like a colonel among troops
crowded into a pair of yellow-chalked
military zones. He's talking strategy.
He's talking peace in the Middle East.
Just as I'm thinking *air strike*,
a rogue flock descends, breaks my concentration
and the colonel's—

but commotion or no,
still nothing here but the blinking cursor
where a poem should've been.
Still nothing but me,
reading metaphors into everything,
time being a luxury I can afford.
Taking it, kneading it, stretching it out.
And why deprive myself?
I like my wily council of birds.
I like that they come to see me now and again.
What else can I do, a writer who writes all day,
my entire studio hemorrhaging light?

The sun beats down
with an exaggerated sense of importance,

        because there aren't any sweet-eyed kids
scampering sweaty and barefoot
through the kitchen. There are no unmade beds,
no rumpled towels on the bathroom floor.
There's no husband,
no dog or cat to care for.
No caged, smart-mouthed parrot slung over a lake
of its own droppings.

It glows this way because it can.

## Objects of Desire

When the ocean calls
When her eye pressed against the window
gives a seismic gasp

When she vows she'll never abandon him
but withholds all sustenance

When he stumbles vacantly about the house
growing fat and middle-aged

When objects of desire
surge, defiantly

      and I'm not talking about the holy or the profane

Water will, from everywhere, storm the gates.

# The Holocaust Tower

You lost your glasses at the Jewish Museum.
Autumn trees were unseasonably bright,
the plazas a patchwork of knackwurst
and graffiti, beer and bicycles and surreal
collectibles of days gone by:
gas masks, canisters, helmets and arm bands,
the rare and the not-so-rare.
Items from the Cold War
in their original boxes.
Everything else was uber-real.
Real coffee to go.
Real people from everywhere,
waving their art around.

Three days we watched poetry films
from Norway, Canada, Egypt,
pixilated worlds composed and decomposed
in fifteen minutes or less,
the time it took the froth to settle on our coffee.
It's what happened afterward.
We were looking deeply into the eyes
of the oven-bound—
great, gaunt sockets. It was there, I think.
Neither of us noticed. Somehow your glasses fell
unannounced into the quiet sweep of tourists.

Or we were too focused
on the darkness at the end of the hall,
the absolute void of a stilled pavilion,
which lured me but swallowed you whole,
your silhouette disappearing
into the matrix of '44,
where your mother shivered inside a cattle car,
World War II exploding overhead.

Later, we found you a new pair.

## The Morning After

Looking past your head at miraculous dawn—
the winnowed lake, enlivened crickets crimping the air—

      how is the rest even possible?

Yesterday's news showed a baleful moon
      in a desert longitude,

reflected in the blood of a Faithful Son

whose fury hurled him skyward
into the face of Allah

      and scattered him like car parts across the Homeland.

I tell you.
The universe wasn't born
      a sinister ball of embroiled asteroids.
People weren't always sick with desire.
Or perhaps they were, but hid it up their sleeve—

What I thought was lilac is the oncoming rain.

I might have only imagined you
      in my bed today.

# Everything Reminds Me of Lolita (H.H.)

(*On the train*)

Evacuation procedures:

Locate end doors and pull to open.
(Part her legs, her divine legs.)

Locate breakout windows.
(Her bare knees, her quivering mouth.)

Break glass with hammer.
(Offer everything, your heart, your throat,
your entrails, let her hold in her awkward fist
the remarkable sceptre of your passion.)

Exit calmly.

Tampering or unauthorized use,
except in case of emergency, is punishable
by fine and/or imprisonment.

 　　　　*

(*Sunday stroll*)

Brown rose, striped shadows.
I see what I see:

skeletal light
along the pebbled road;

a spiny trail
of pine cones trampled into spiders,
but so much more . . .
delectable—

one
in particular, a rogue,
its splayed limbs
shaped like an X,

like a sleeping child
across her tousled bed,
the prickly sunlight
grazing her vertebrae.

## Street Performer

The fun of being a child and pretty and alive
is not what she considers fun.
The sacrosanct male need:
bees and nectar, the unsavoury mess
of the sweet-scented woods behind her house—
earth, water, fruit.
The eyes that behold her, and linger.

In the pure morning distance,
she is a sting of light.

She balances on a beach ball in her pinstripes
and polka dots.
Any minute now, she could tumble.
Children are laughing.
People on their way to work
are dropping coins into her droopy hat.

## Gaping Breach of Propriety

Light on his feet, he salutes the day
with a boy's sense of its faceted treasures,
which he can name:

Hello *city*! Hello *sky*!
He walks with moxy. Struts.

Hello *arteries*! Hello *veins*!

      Hey, you over there—*Mister*!

Mister moves at an ominous clip,
a concentrated field of energy.
The world has its fingers crossed.

It hopes the child remembers
what's been taught,
despite the sweet-talking brain:
*Never chase a bouncing ball into the road.*

Because at the vanishing point—
      and everyone knows this—
the man will disappear,
and that tantalizing package under his arm—

it could power an earthquake
or send shimmering projectiles
hurtling into the stratosphere.

## The Glass Half Empty

Things were better in the '40s.
But I'm not saying *go back*.
To bread and blackstrap molasses
cramping the cupboards
of a town where beastly winds
rip houses off their foundations;
where a mother, pregnant
for the tenth time, spears long johns
in a galvanized tub of lye,
dips her long-handled fork
into the steam and scoops
"dem jeesus tings" up for inspection
before dropping them
back down into the slop;
a woman in the half light
bent over cloudy wash water.
I'm not saying that.

I meant the '50s,
when winds colder than Moscow
shot through our school.
The key was not to faint
but to remain inert
under our desks, imagining
the fallout of an asteroid
half the size of a hockey rink.
We didn't really think of dying.
But the newsreel looped
through the spools of our brains,
numbing us until the '60s,
when a flash of insight
equivalent to a thousand A-bombs
detonated over an entire
g-g-generation,
and what we saw, Christ, what we saw
of human waste was more than . . .

I might have been thinking of the '70s.
Or the '80s, or '90s,
or even the first dubious hours
of this millennium—

sometimes I think cellphones suck
more than anything.

# Thoughts After Another Explosion in Aleppo

Nothing anymore is innocuous.
An aphid on a single leaf

blights an entire garden.
The encroaching days are deliberate

and heavily perfumed, and have little to do
with our summers of excess,

when the casual breeze lifted our hair.
I remember us as we were then—

rain-soaked kids in yellow galoshes,
exuberance pouring from our lips.

I remember Cracker Jacks surprises
and starlight ricocheting off rooftops

when toys with pull strings and windup
hearts had yet to be been invented.

## Boy with Lego

He sprawls in a panel of light, each piece of his kingdom
      lined up and colour-coded,
            and God help the guy who tells him
that life isn't what it's cracked up to be.

Not everyone teetering
      on a lonely bridge
            comes out as lucky as Job.
But that's his discovery.

I'm the mother. I anticipate the shadows
      that feast on unsuspecting little boys.
            It's my job. To see, beyond the open blind,
the carnivorous gaze of the city.

Down the road, a leashed dog with a boulder-sized
      head and the canines of a wolf
            is biding its time,
squatting over the grass to pee.

            For now, stasis.

The sun crashing in is hardly a horned beast
      with a flaming tail. The world is as it should be,
            the constant sky beyond the linden tree and
a glee-eyed child charging up his cavalry.

## The Devil in the Details

Because the Towers fell, because we're paranoid
about the chariot of unattended luggage,
the carload of Arabs hurrying to the border,

we treat the scribbled graffiti
above the urinal at McDonald's
like Exhibit A in a court case,
or a hefty metaphor.

Suspicions rush to configure themselves:
an unnamed warehouse
filled with dynamite. Elsewhere,
minding its own business, the target.

The mind races to fill in the gaps,
but no skyscraper this time,
no congested hub. Just a hillside barn.
A grey-planked affair
with a few side teeth knocked out.

We imagine how the sky will appear,
tinged violet, when a dark vibration
reaches a nest of swallows tucked
in the rafters; the sweet-smelling hay,

ominous stillness.
Within that stillness, an effervescence—trapped
particles of dust in a sunbeam, waiting for something
both micro- and macroscopic to occur.

## Morning with Paintbrush

The umber wave of morning heaved—
I felt nausea only.
Outside, in tatters:
the exhausted grass, gnarled
trees,
in sickly greys.
I painted.
I painted as the sky choked and summer drained
through the cooling soil. I painted through the ghoulish
season of pumpkins and corn husks, through hoarfrost;
I painted as the dark snow left handprints
on our windows.
Colour returned me to the earth.

The painting intensified—
through the exhaust of cars and their alarming
headlights. I painted as the gunman entered
through an emergency door no one had locked.
I painted through the sirens and ambulances,
through news bulletins and the steady rain
of bullets. I painted as the children hid
under chalkboards and chairs.
As the universe tried to tell me
over and over again, there are two sorts of human.
One is relentless. He sees in his fervour
what he chooses to see.

ii

## Post-mortem

I got your letter. It wasn't much of a letter.
I should have listened to common sense
and left it on the credenza.
But as Oscar Wilde said, I can resist everything
except temptation.

It ruined my night. All your talk
about the tragic dimensions of love

reminded me of the brain's criss-crossing pathways;
the submolecular accidents and collisions
that once put us in the right place
at the right time
when we might well have been
dining in different time zones.

Or arguing, as usual, about the wine.

I was the pleasure seeker and you—
you salivated over spreadsheets
and insurance policies, the Dow and the TSX.
So, gridlock. If only—

If only you'd embraced the curled-up worm
at the base of your skull, ignored the Executive cortex,
traded the business suit for a place
among our scaly ancestors.

Our neural wiring kept defeating us.
The heart, to be honest, was irrelevant.

## School

The child slides down the long neck of the week into Friday. Slouched
at his desk he has a target on his forehead. The teacher wants an answer.
He shrugs it off, the way he shrugs off his backpack. All this energy,
trapped inside him, biding its time, waiting for him to shed his chrysalis.
Quietly he floats in the canoe of thought, moved by its gentle ebb and
flow. Downwind, familiar sounds: the plash of a cast-off net, a fish hook
trembling over spangled water. It is mid-morning there, but over here the
teacher keeps at him, as though his brain were a cabbage she is helping
to grow. Smiling but firm, she says encouraging things like "Shoot for
the moon—even if you miss, you'll land among the stars." He wishes
she would see that he is not a dwarf planet. If she cared an iota, she'd
know about the swirl and eddy of life around him, starting with his
grandfather's cabin and the long blue arms of the sky. He knows from
memory the music of frisky mosquitoes and snapping twigs.

Everything he needs is in the physics of the moving water, translucent
with fish.

## Study of My Son Doing Homework

Calculus focuses you, whittles your attention
to a point and arrests time—or makes it
or breaks it, or adds to it,
or subtracts from it, or divides it by
the serious square root of two.
One way or the other, it engineers time.

Number strings float across your laptop
like flotsam and jetsam,
saturating the screen with nebulous possibility.
Your best work occurs from midnight to 3:00 a.m.
Teachers praise your intellect.
I'm your mother, what can I say?
I may know jack about math, but this I do know:

your scribbles lure you down a rabbit hole
caked with the dirt of the daunting playground,
where each day, each week,
year after year, the bullies took turns
swiping your tuque. Footballed it back and forth
over the winter snow while your chubby fists
pummelled the air
haplessly. But now, metaphorically,
the tables are turned on the oversized oafs,
all three lying, beaten, across the spring dreck.

I gather this is how it is
when hatred and determination intersect
in a quintessential particle of the brain:
You locate a point in the house
where you can spread out and think,
moonlight grazing your cheek.
The kitchen's a good bet, and why not?
A tall glass of milk and your cookies of choice
wait on the table.
On the wall, your diploma of excellence.

And this, not the old look of fright,
is the last image I have of you
before turning in at night:
you solving for x.

Chewing your pencil,
tilting your head from side to side
as a solution,
like the blue seep of ink through a page,
begins to reveal itself.

## Where Night Takes Me

There's no pinning down what resists
pinning down:
       boys, at 16, want the keys to the car.
Clear nights, starry nights, stormy nights.
Stormy nights.
They're indestructible.

As I was, decades ago, while my mother
hovered in the drapes, clutching her rosary.
She'd slipped St. Christopher
into the glove compartment.

Tonight, in all this rain, it's me who's obsessing.
Eyeball to eyeball with the heartless universe.

What upsets me, aside from death itself,
is what we settle for—not the sun's cruel core
but a cloudy promise that God will go to bat for us,
no matter what. He'll strong-arm
our malicious, misguided opponents.
If only we believe.

But the unknowns keep piling up.

I've no idea what it is to be moss or jade
in the spectrum of green. There are no patterns;
there is no good light to measure anything by.
The laws of physics drop like an ax.

In the end, the body doesn't keep.

# Pathology Report 1

*Clinical Information*:
invasive lobular carcinoma & radial scar

1. right axilla, sentinel lymph node #1, count: 1848, excision
2. skin tag, excision

3. right breast, needle-localized segmental mastectomy
4. right breast, new lateral margin (blue), excision

*Specimen*:
I found you as I knew I would

1. portly hips filling an upholstered chaise
2. in an airy room of lilac & sun

3. the bloom of your cigarette now a downturned
4. worm, hanging by a thread

## The Gene

The grim, hospital-gowned women
want the facts. Who are you?
How did you get here?
They fear you as others feared Hitler or Stalin
or the Ayatollah, fathers
of some of the meanest vectors of poison.

But what match are they for your diabolical wit?
You, the prime architect
of the scariest, subatomic piranha
in history.

Okay.
Let's not, as people say, get ahead of ourselves.

You're what the mind makes of you
on a still day,
under a bright swipe of sky
while the kid next door goes haywire,
spray-painting the garden chairs
with indelible ink—

the elephant in the room,
the pea under the mattress,
that one niggling thing.

You're the epic hanger-on
after the last trees have been stripped bare.
The party straggler
walking around with his shirt undone
and a cognac in his hand.
Clearly, he isn't leaving anytime soon.

# Diptych

Before I can say yes or no with any degree of clarity,
she is loosening her blouse, snipping away layers
of hospital gauze.

And the child inside me, who delighted
in strapping firecrackers to the helpless backs of frogs
because of an elevated tolerance for gore
(and, yes, because I could) is wildly euphoric,

while my older, more finicky self wants something
sugar-coated: a Catholic wafer dipped in wine,
or Tinkerbell. Or rainbow fish beneath
a glass-bottomed boat.
Sun-filled ones, not the kind that cannibalize their young
in the fight to survive.

&#42;

Both worshipping and cursing the impressive
instruments of technology, the husband's imagination
blooms in the days following his wife's mastectomy—

call it obsessive, call it the soup of too many pills,
prescription and otherwise.
Not an endless night of counting sheep,
but close.
The sharklike mind circling the same thoughts:

glutinous rain forests,
radioactive lagoons of bubbled-up waste.
The jackhammered city,
gashed and rutted as the moon beyond the lace curtain
of the window he turns toward, in bed.

# Pathology Report 2

*I believe that I am in hell, therefore I am there.*
—Arthur Rimbaud

This is not a crime scene.
But examine the overturned chair
on the floor, impossibly angled,
your whitish arms in the abundant sunlight.
Note the blond wig and headscarf
you wore daily. Trying to keep your secret
secret.

All you ever wanted: to hold yourself so still
that nothing escapes.

Not a crime scene,
but your spiral into the vortex
of worst-case scenarios.
Listen for the maudlin violins.
Someone in the audience is crying.
Symptoms you don't have names for
are climbing out of your dancing shoes.

The blue is telling. So's the prognosis.
The shoes are blue. The shoes,
according to your file, are pointed west.

## Letter to Albert

First, it was the last rites,
then the cadenced lull after that storm knocked
the socks off Montreal, Toronto,
Ottawa and Prince Edward Island.

You in your death wrap are oblivious.
Everything bright is covered in snow.

I want to apologize for the impoverished day.
So little to point to
            to honour your leaving.
Except maybe the apple on my desk,
strangely radiant in its rinse of light.

## Upon Seeing *Life of Pi* on the Eve of the Eve of your Death

Even in the movie theatre, I wonder
what your eye takes in as night slides down,
dissolving your world.
Are you already thinking, *This is it?*
There it goes, slipping away,
a parade turning the corner,
marching bands and baton-twirling majorettes
taking with them all their pomp and circumstance.

I watched the countdown, the accumulated
panic in your brow, your family waiting
as time struggled on, the sum total of everything
beyond the hospital
flourishing, cities and forests and oceans
regenerating themselves by the minute.
Now I'm here, eating popcorn.

Epicurus might have been right:
we are nothing, we are, we are not, we don't care.
The coffin lid drops and everything, I mean everything,
stops—right there.

But, honestly? Hope tastes better to me:
the idea of me on a boat
with a Bengal tiger, by ourselves
except for maybe a meddlesome God perched
on a cloud close by, for good measure.

Just above that spot where the channel
empties into the sea.

## The Hottest Car I Ever Drove Was a 1978 Monza with a V8 Engine and a Fuchsia Interior

But my nose, today, is in a novel
about an adulterous queen in her canopy bed.
Two-thirds in, I'm at the juicy bit,
where finally, after the light grazes
her shapely thigh,
after a life of slavish devotion to things,
she runs a simple comb through her lover's locks.

The lover is no porcelain doll.
She is a woman.
She burns
with every kind of unsettling weather.

The queen, however? Ambivalent.

"A single wind sends a boat adrift. And yet
it returns," she says. "The world is awry.
Desire, lust—neither of these
can set anything straight."

In fact, she understands little
except that time's always existed, and once
every few moons,
the sky balloons, vermilion.

I sort of know where this is going.

Like a leaf, she'll disintegrate into a thing
too small to name. Then she'll be shameless
about slipping off her silk bodice and surrendering.
She'll make a lover of night.

This, it seems to me, is a glimpse into God.

# How God Looked in My Dream

A gentleman's gentleman, he reviles the tourist traps
in the prairies, in the desert,
along the scalloped shores of the Atlantic
and in the shaded foothills of the bluish mountains.

The bawdy atmosphere
nauseates him: motor courts slung with air freshener,
honky-tonk campgrounds wired to the Internet.
I could go on ad infinitum,

substituting one U-shaped paradise for another:
Kozy Kabins; rustic lakeside lodges
of knotty pine and chenille bedspreads, where a quarter
dropped through a slot turns an impotent mattress
into a bucking, nostril-flaring bronco;

pink-and-white ruffled inns with ruffled pillows
and matching Kleenex boxes; rest stops with ice machines
and mini-bars, candy dispensers
in every dingy, bulb-lit hall.
Memory Lane Apartments. The Sunset Motel.

But I digress.

This particular mensch settles into the posh interior
of the Waldorf Astoria Hotel,
properly tuxedoed
and neckerchiefed with the finest linen serviette.

Between courses, *entre le soupe du jour et le trou normand*,
as a heaping slice of his face stares back at him
from the glittering silverware, he scratches his head,
lights a cigar like Scott Fitzgerald,
and goes about the tall business of scribbling
onto pigskin his unprecedented ideas for a Book.

## Garbage Day Meditation

In the grainy light, it looks a lot worse
than it probably is, lying there,
face down on the curb, exposed backside
a coil of broken anatomy:
crushed vertebrae, some intestinal wiring.
The thin shadow of death has settled.

I feel a pang of longing for the four-legged
console of my youth,
whose snowy signal delivered soap flakes
and Ed Sullivan into our living room—
until a creeping Cancer metastasized into
the Cuban Missile Crisis,
and Jack Ruby's nefarious bullet
burned through the fey musculature
of a most un-presidential man.

It's my earliest memory:
Mother starching Father's shirts.
Horrified, I watched as the bulging eye
of our television flashed a hatful of night.

## Dinner Party

I want to say to our host uncorking the Merlot
he's dead right about the narrow channels
of the human mind.
Another guest drifts back into the conversation:
"I assume you mean our federal politicians?"
So earnest with his olive branch.
But already we are on to common stupidity, vice,
the banal human crimes of our century.

We apologize to no one in particular
for the discombobulated ecosystem, chastise
the ancient woolly tribes who began on the right foot
but trampled the grassy goodness
in their protracted spread across the globe.

"Here, here," goes Olive Branch, waving his Scotch.
"Did we learn nothing from the Titanic?"

Our woozy meanderings keep us afloat
until a waterfall of laughter cascades
from somebody's Wife Number Three,
with dazzling toenails and lipstick to match.
Her mouth opens wider than her handbag—
"Funny, up until last week, I thought Dhaka was in Germany . . ."

A monumental hush falls over us.
The flickering darkness of a power surge,
a sudden drop in wattage.
It is so quiet
I can hear the rasping filaments of every light bulb.
When the refrigerator comes back on,
everyone's talking at once again.

# 5:00 a.m. the Day of Your Mother's Funeral

—FOR T.K.

If the day can't stand at half-mast,
it should remain, at the very least,
in partial shadow.
Only the barest inkling
of sun on the horizon.
Dwindling poplars should lament
the night's bitter aftertaste.

I'm headed east
in the florid darkness of a motor coach
shaped like a bullet, long and silver,
with passing flashes
through the windows—

showy billboards advertising carry-on luggage
for "that trip of a lifetime,"
cars with their receding tail lights
floating down the highway.

The world should stay this way the entire day:
dusky, sleepy, nothing its true colour;
the sky washed out
or sealed in an atmospheric coma.

When I blink again, clouds become the haunches
of an Arctic wolf advancing on its prey.
And what I take for the scattering light—

it's the charged particle of a wilful star
severing ties with the earth.

## Night Drive

As a child, I wondered about the muted lamplight
of the homes we passed as winter blazed.
The trick was not to fall asleep but to notice everything
in its brevity,
to catch the fleeting details of this or that:
a widow in a black dress, folded in on herself;
the wire hook on a naked wall
where someone's photograph has been taken down;
       little hatching signs of spring—
a gutter's teary icicle,
Mother inhaling deeply, singing,
"She'll be comin' 'round the mountain when she comes . . ."

Once while we were driving, the darkness splintered
into a million shards. Apparently we had struck a moose.
For weeks afterwards, I couldn't go near the basement.
The groaning furnace terrified me.

It is not a parenthetical world out there.
There is no simple way, for anyone, to go on.

# Barkwoodby

—AFTER THE PAINTING "ABOVE LAKE SUPERIOR," BY LAWREN HARRIS

Nunced clouds in five shades of hawtone.
An acqualous sky.
Skinny birches, brittier than most,
amburned by sun.

And voila, the first surprise of spring:
shadows following the early snow,
gnarly roots of a snaking momonon.

The rest, you anticipate:
                    cherry blossoms,
giddened chuts of light,
scrots and dreaks of runnah.
All whispering
their emplet of solitude.

You've read Thoreau.
You recognize these pabled woods,
the moratern bludge
at the heart of every mountain
echoing its name.

# Note
Tempera on Yellow Post-it
76 x 76 mm
(c. 2007)


You asked what I wanted this year
and I wrote "a cure,"
meaning any of the gruelling roads ahead.
Give me colicky seasons
and barbarian wind,
a writhing snake pit of stars.

What I want?

The weedy landscape
to collapse under the total sum of our being.

Earthquakes and flash floods,
the unstoppable melt
of the dwindling glaciers.

I want you to take my hand and walk me
into the hurricane.

## Introduction to Reiki

I wasn't, as they say, in the centre
of my life. But neither was anyone else
in the room,
chakras as clogged as our kitchen sinks.
We sat on the floor in stocking feet,
the Great Lotus filling our lungs.

One spoke of a churning
in her solar plexus,
another complained of a constant buzzing.
　　　On her wedding night,
she'd waltzed with her mate
under the fiery stars as cosmic debris
slid off them like rain.
But, eventually ...

How people repeat the same mistakes,
was what we were thinking.
How a wife becomes a woman trapped
inside a radioactive cloud.
The Master twirled his wand of incense,
lifting our spirits.
My arches rooted to the ground.

It could have been a different weekend.
I could have been home in my slippers,
watching the Middle East self-destruct.
Maybe I'd have broken down—
or swept out my garage.
Or caught the airwaves issuing a ceasefire
as the Earth's plates shifted to a halt.

This isn't so much about growth as a door
swinging open on the almost-dead.

## Daybreak, Georgian Bay

A mole by the side of the road
lies dead.
Flat as a mango's anatomical bone.
A humble thing,
definitively extinguished.

Its shirked-open mouth
points up at the sky.
An abyss, an entryway
dark as the earth itself, gleaming
with unborn effulgence.

Somewhere, peripherally, a sun.

Noises, too, distant at first.
Shiftings and stirrings
beyond the broad-leafed trees:

a fawn, a cottage
with a red-sloped roof,
children.
Just another few steps
to the jubilant crickets
and the fluid, lake-steeped
horizon.

## Watching You Do Tai Chi at Dawn

There's a burgeoning gap in the sky
as the clouds part above you,
in a distant realm
where sea lice and the latrine stench
of declining civilizations are virtually non-existent.
And like me, you're here,
but somehow you're not.

What I admire is not you
or the hulking freighter of what you know;
what's awesome is your coexistence
with the flea-sized minutiae of the galaxy—
you, graceful as a gull,
the perfectly stilled world
in your gaze.

It could be any day, but it's Friday.
Tomorrow we return to the city.
And so I study you
as an artist scans the planes and curves
of a partially lit stone.
But there's no great revelation.

The earth doesn't shake or rumble
with meaning as a rosy light settles
over the beach.

       There's just one crested wave.
And then another, and another.

# Notes

"Space" was inspired by the events surrounding the alleged abuse of a two-year-old Edmonton girl by her parents in 2012.

The cento "Collage" was collaged out of bits and pieces—sometimes verbatim, sometimes adapted—from the following:

*Abraham*, Colin Browne (Brick Books, 1987)

*Simple Master*, Alice Burdick (Pedlar Press, 2002)

*Renga*, Patrick Deane, Peggy Dragisic, Sheila McColm, David White (Brick Books, 1981)

New work by Jeramy Dodds in *Syd & Shirley*, issue #1

*This Woman Alphabetical*, Laura Farine (Pedlar Press, 2005)

*Steam-Cleaning Love*, J. A. Hamilton (Brick Books, 1993)

*Walking into the Night Sky*, Lyn King (Brick Books, 2002)

*Radio Picasso*, Steve McCabe (Watershed Books, 1999)

*Slant*, Andy Quan (Nightwood Editons, 2001)

*Farmer Gloomy's New Hybrid*, Stuart Ross (ECW Press, 1999)

*Hey Crumbling Balcony!: Poems New and Selected*, Stuart Ross (ECW Press, 2003)

"Stub's Wife" by Barbara Simler in *Arc Poetry Magazine*, Summer 2005

*Slow-Moving Target*, Sue Wheeler (Brick Books, 2000)

"Figure and Ground" was adapted from the short film *Léger Problème* (2009) by Hélène Florent.

"Colour" is a riff on a line from *How Fiction Works* (Farrar, Straus and Giroux, 2008) by James Wood.

"Morning with Paintbrush" was composed one week before the Sandy Hook Elementary School shooting, which occurred on December 14, 2012.

The Epicurus quotation referred to in "Upon Seeing *Life of Pi* on the Eve of the Eve of your Death" was adapted for the poem. The original words are: "I was not, I was, I am not, I care not."

"Barkwoodby" is a tribute to Lewis Carroll and employs nonsense words randomly generated by the computer.

# Acknowledgements

Thanks to the editors of the following publications where some poems, or versions of them, first appeared: *Poetry Quebec*, *CV2*, and the *Literary Review of Canada*.

A multidisciplinary performance of "City of Everything" took place on April 26, 2013 at the Bain St. Michel in Montreal, featuring the author, Endre Farkas, Jean René and Vicki Tansey.

Special thanks to the team at Brick, and to my editor, Sue Sinclair, for her tireless work and commitment; to Diane Shaker for offering me the Georgian Bay cottage for an intense week of writing; and to Alex for his constant, loving support. Gratitude and more to Endre Farkas, my partner in life and art, who read the early manuscript and provided incisive feedback.

CAROLYN MARIE SOUAID is the Montreal-based author of six previous books of poetry and the editor of over a dozen. She has toured her work across Canada, Europe and the U.S., and has been shortlisted for a number of literary awards including the A. M. Klein Prize for Poetry and the Pat Lowther Memorial Award. In 2012, her videopoem, *Blood is Blood*, won a prize at the ZEBRA Poetry Film Festival in Berlin.

From 2008 to 2011, she served as poetry editor for Signature Editions. In 2009, she co-founded *Poetry Quebec*, the first online review showcasing the English-language poetry and poets of Quebec. In 2013, she was awarded a seven-week writer's residency at the Banff Centre to work on a novel.

Souaid holds an M. A. in Creative Writing from Concordia University.